ABOUT THE AUTHOR

Jemima Hughes is a mental health and sexual violence awareness activist and multi slam winning performance poet. Jemima's debut poetry collection *Unorthodox*, published with Verve Poetry Press in 2020, challenges perceptions of living with sexual trauma and mental health difficulties. This second collection *Into The Ordinary* aims to change perspectives on how we can make the world a more accepting, understanding and comfortable place for those living with these experiences. Jemima takes you on a journey through her own experiences, providing a relatable outlet and encouraging conversation.

Unorthodox was what happened. *Into The Ordinary* explores what we can do about it.

Jemima has had multiple features on BBC upload, BBC radio Coventry and Warwickshire, Black Country Radio Xtra and Hillz FM. Her headline performances have taken her all over the UK and Ireland to poetry events and music festivals including Stendhal Festival 2019, BBC Contains Strong Language 2022, Shambala Festival 2023 and Moseley Folk Festival 2023. Jemima has headlined shows online streaming all over the world to countries including Canada, the United States, Pakistan and Australia. Her work is published in numerous anthologies including *We've Done Nothing Wrong, We've Nothing To Hide* with Verve Poetry Press and *The Scriptstuff Lockdown Anthology*. She's been published in magazines including *Steel Jackdaw* and *Shine Magazine* in association with the Women's Awards. Jemima was longlisted for the Outspoken Prize For Poetry 2023.

As a believer that listening saves lives, more recently Jemima has turned her hand to hosting, aiming to provide the same opportunity of being heard to others that they have provided to her.

A list of support resources can be found at:
www.jemimahughespoet.co.uk/support.

Social media:
Instagram @jemima_unspoken
Facebook @jemima_unspoken
Youtube: https://www.youtube.com/c/UnorthodoxJemima/videos
Website: www.jemimahughespoet.co.uk
TikTok: @jemima_unspoken

Jemima Hughes
Into The Ordinary

VERVE
POETRY PRESS
BIRMINGHAM

PUBLISHED BY VERVE POETRY PRESS
https://vervepoetrypress.com
mail@vervepoetrypress.com

All rights reserved
© 2023 Jemima Hughes

The right of Jemima Hughes to be identified as author of this work has been asserted in accordance with section 77 of the Copyright, Designs and Patents Act 1988.

No part of this work may be reproduced, stored or transmitted in any form or by any means, graphic, electronic, recorded or mechanical, without the prior written permission of the publisher.

FIRST PUBLISHED JULY 2023

Printed and bound in the UK
by ImprintDigital, Exeter

ISBN: 978-1-913917-40-1
eBook: 978-1-913917-82-1

Cover Photograph by Tim Horgan

To anyone who has been made to feel like they're out of the ordinary for having natural responses to life events.

To anyone who has been made to feel blame or shame for situations out of their control.

This book is for you and me.

Look after you, you're important.

CONTENTS

Together #1	11
Childhood Delusion	12
Together #2	13
Jemanji	14
Together #3	20
7: Occasional 1	21
Together #4	27
His Name Is...	28
Together #5	32
Jordan Boyd	33
Together #6	36
I'm Talking To You	37
Together #7	39
Friends	40
Together #8	46
Did I?	47
Together #9	49
Self-Sabotage	50
Stars	50
Together #10	51
Train	52
Together #11	59
Tiffany	60

Together #12	65
Shakespeare	66
Together #13	72
Communication Is Sexy And Consent Is Compulsory	74
Together #14	80
Defining Moment	81
Together #15	86
Dust	87
Together #16	91
Road To Anywhere	92
Together #17	94
Dear Men	95
Together #18	100
Kintsugi	101
Bravery	101
Together #19	102
Every Woman Who's Ever Been Abused...	103
Together #20	109
This Is Not A Motivational Speech	110
You	117

A Hill I Won't Die On - *James Scott-Howes*
Metaphormosis - *Claire Tedstone*

Acknowledgements & Credits

Into The Ordinary

Together #1

I don't do small talk.
Let's think big.
Dig
deep.
Find gold
and share it with everyone around us.

Childhood Delusion

Age 12 she was called names because she was the quiet child
but she wasn't bullied
and she still smiled
because those sorts of things don't happen to people like her.

Age 14 she was restricting her meals
but her eating wasn't disordered
and she wasn't trying to conceal
because those sorts of things don't happen to people like her.

Age 16 she was sexually abused
but she wasn't raped
and her body wasn't used
because those sorts of things don't happen to people like her.

Age 18 her best friend was killed
but she didn't register his loss
and she didn't have to rebuild
because those sorts of things don't happen to people like her.

Age 25 she had a mental breakdown,
gasping for air she felt like she was going to drown
in the build-up of lessons life cruelly felt she should own,
her smile was dragged into the deepest frown.

Emotions escalated when she was told to calm down,
streets felt empty as she walked through the busy town,
she lost her glow for which she was once renowned,
trapped in the darkness, light couldn't be found.

Because those sorts of things,
all of those sorts of things,
can happen to anyone.

Together #2

Some days, I look at my reflection and I smile.
I see a glimpse of the girl who grew with no worries
of what life would ever be.
She would always be
happy.

I stopped
looking for answers in old photographs
and started looking in the mirror,
caught up with myself.
Some days my reflection is more back to front, on others it's clearer.

Jemanji

It's all fun and games
until the game comes to life,
until the chest is more than a sight to behold,
one that opens to expose a psychologist's paradise.

It's more than the image that fronts the box
that made you believe getting involved would be alright
or the words that warned you not to play
but still left you enticed.

This world is magical, supernatural, unimaginable
until the challenge lays right before your eyes
and your next move is as uncertain
as the next roll of a dice.

The one to inflict this pursuit on me
left me alone to fend
but following situations I've had to see,
fear has become my friend,

pain has become a reason to succeed,
not a means to an end.
I'm lost, but knowing what's coming up next
is even harder to comprehend.

Who needs an imagination with multiple realities?
Sometimes things will go awry,
I've known occurrences to be life threatening
but I'm not afraid to die.

I'm afraid that I'm not afraid to die.

I'm protective of the chaos,
it's the only way I know.
I don't want you to leave but wouldn't blame you if you did
so this is your chance to go.

"A game for those who seek to find,
a way to leave their world behind."
Yours will perish when ours entwine,
I'm not keeping you here, our movements are magnetised.

You watch your back, I'll watch mine,
we can still be allies
but to reach our full potential
single player is advised.

The reality is, I'm not a nightmare
or a dream.
I'm a reality
under fantasy's disguise.

How does it feel
to unintentionally take a turn?
You get sucked in, you try to resist,
then to the jungle you must adjourn,

it reminds you that you're mortal
as you search for ways for it to be reversed,
I've spent years within this wild life,
there's still parts I'm yet to learn.

"At night they fly, you better run,
these winged things are not much fun."
They come alive in the darkness,
they've taught me to succumb

but I've learnt to adapt my limbs as wings
to rise above obstacles one by one
and if I don't cave during the longest nights,
the morning light will always come.

I've spent too many hours in therapy
convinced they're a hallucination,
that something so radical must be made up
but they're a legitimate obligation.

"A tiny bite can make you itch,
make you sneeze, make you twitch."

Hundreds of antennae heighten my senses,
I continuously switch
between smell, touch, taste, hearing,
each one experiencing a glitch.

Hairs and goosebumps start to rise,
the crawling is about to begin,
they're piercing through my comfort zone,
drawing blood from beneath my skin.

I'm an out-of-control freak
with skin that crawls like forest ground,
I'm always prepared and it's made my skin thicker,
I keep moving with my chin up and my head down.

I don't reside in a place where one was murdered,
I adventure where a survivor has been nurtured,
it's okay to be afraid that the fantasy is becoming absurd,
I know you're considering leaving after the calamities that
    have occurred.

The rules say if we finish the game it will all go away
but the deadline is blurred,

I told you I didn't need your help,
that it's much more fun to observe.

Or did I fool you into coming with the way I used my words?

"This will not be an easy mission,
monkeys slow the expedition."

All up in my business,
exploiting my condition,
unimpressed if their manipulation
doesn't lure me into submission.

They swing through the memories behind my eyes
leaving me blind to what the game has designed
and to what is authentic,
undermining my everyday grind.

They've taught me that when life hands you bananas,
be patient whilst they become ripe,
share them when they're easier to digest
and their benefits can be refined.

I don't need protecting. I've been there,
I'm still here, taking steps to prevent deterioration,
don't feel sorry that I'm trapped,
open your mind to this unfathomable creation.

"His fangs are sharp, he likes your taste,
your party better move. Poste haste."

I locked him in my heart
the first time we came tooth to face,
partly for his bravery,
partly to fill the empty space.

Now he doesn't let anyone else in
and you're trying to take his place,
I don't know if he makes me strong or numb
but he keeps my tribal beat at a steady pace.

"They grow much faster than bamboo,
take care or they'll come after you."

The walls you've built,
they're about to crash through,
your foundations are trembling,
I'll share techniques to ground you.

I'd learnt not to overanalyse
to avoid unnecessary pain,
now my safe space is compromised
by an animal control problem I'm struggling to tame.

"Don't be fooled, it isn't thunder,
staying put would be a blunder."

There's a massive elephant in the room,
carrying great weight and filling you with wonder,
don't ask questions you don't want answers to,
the stampede of sensations could take you under.

"Every month at the quarter moon,
there will be a monsoon in your lagoon."

I'm a natural disaster waiting to happen,
the storm will pass over soon,
you worry when I cry but it reminds me I'm alive,
high ground doesn't make you immune.

"Beware of the ground on which you stand,
the floor is quicker than the sand."

Don't struggle against your reservations,
reach out and take my hand,
the grounding techniques I taught you
will get you back on familiar land.

"Need a hand? Well you just wait,
we'll help you out, we each have eight."

You don't know who's reaching out,
we're an equation you're trying to calculate
but none of us are dangerous
and our touch is always delicate.

"You're almost there with much at stake,
now the ground begins to quake."
The commotion is causing your head to ache,
you're exhausted from all the hours spent awake.

If I stepped back, would you step forward to close the gap
or would you take the break?
You're becoming distant, it's okay, it's time to go,
bringing you in was my mistake.

Living this way is painful enough
without feeling bad for living this way.
This is the only life I have to offer you,
you've reached the end of play.

I don't want to live like this
but I need to be approached without a content warning.
I've tried to change and realised this is my only option.
And maybe, it will never be enough.

Or maybe, it will always be too much.

Together #3

When the colour drained from my eyes
it flooded under my skin,
inflicting pain to relieve pain,
I can't remember the last time I didn't have a headache
from my patience wearing thin.

I will hurt myself
before I'm close enough to lay even a breath on your skin,
there may be no excuse for my reactions
but there is always a reason
and for the love of all the Gods
I don't believe in,
we have to stop judging mental illness
so people stop disappearing.

7: Occasional 1

There's something disorderly
about the way I eat,
you've probably heard of the 5:2
people use to structure their week,

well, I do the 7:occasional 1
to both extremes,
I'm not a fussy eater,
the control is something I seek

or maybe I want to cover as many mental illnesses as I can
before one of them ends my streak,
yes, the lack of nourishment
makes my joints feel antique,

when your mental illness fits you more comfortably than your clothes
and you can hear your mirror shriek
it is easier to feed your obsession
rather than your physique.

I don't own a thigh gap,
I own a pair that clap,
sarcastically, as I run from my responsibilities,
the sound is enough to make me snap,

when you can run from situations
quicker than you can adapt,
running is more appealing
than sticking around for a relapse

of another disorder
you've just managed to grasp,

when conceding to one improves another,
you always feel trapped

and when you don't recognise who you've become,
how are you supposed to recognise how you act?

I can't tell if I'm spiralling
or dizzy from excessive caffeine intake
to keep me going
to keep me awake

because hunger starves you of sleep
as much as everything else on your plate,
forget butterflies, I get bats
whose movements make me shake,

their heightened hearing disturbed by rumbles
inevitably leads to bellyache,
their big appetites request more fulfilment
than I can willingly demonstrate.

They rest in the morning
when the fridge light beckons me in,
I've been lured into places that have left me worse for wear
so milk for a cuppa is all I need to begin.

When starvation sounds like the solution,
you know you've got the problem confused,
it's worrying when the action is wrong
but who you're doing it for is right because you're only doing it
    for you.

I just want to look like I designed me,
not like the girl who's been misused,
I'm not satisfied doing the wrong thing
but trying to fix it leaves me unenthused,

like, potholes under our wheels
lead us all to have a moan
but workers taking up space to fix them
leaves us cursing them to get out of the road,

we want things fixed
without the inconvenience of having to take it slow,
this world is shortcuts, edging into risk
rather than waiting patiently at a crossroad.

It's about finding a balance but when my mind works in extremes,
how can it serve my body in moderation?
The smell of freshly baked bread conjures thoughts of the knife to
    cut it
quicker than the mouth-watering appreciation,

Instagram stories documenting dinners
only fuel my fixation,
friends ask me to do their diets for support,
I'd love to help but my habits are not up for negotiation.

My calendar of green and red crosses
dictates the good days and the bad.
Until now, I've been the only one to know,
red slates me for what I ate and green means no food was had.

The red days are the opposite end of the spectrum,
deprivation turns to demand,
I am ravenous,
my body has taken all it can withstand,

now it hurts to eat.
Or do I eat until it hurts?
Chasing that first-bite high,
each forced mouthful making the pain worse.

The late-night metabolism kick
inflicting nightmares like a curse,
if you un-make your bed you still have to lie in it
with hopes the discomfort will disperse.

Like, drinking a hot drink too soon,
you wait and anticipate the burn,
then the sensation lingers on to remind you
this mishap will take time to reverse.

I used to work as a greengrocer,
I once chased after a man who pocketed one onion with stealth,
if only I cared that much about a piece of food now,
maybe I could improve my health,

instead, I'm slipping through my fingers
like a mango peeled and sliced,
one that from the outside looks full of goodness,
inside is a bruised and feeble sight.

I don't know what game I'm playing with myself
but if this is winning, I should box it up and put it back on the shelf.
This is not a trap I fell into, I jumped when I felt compelled,
these aren't the cards I was handed to play, these are the cards I
        knowingly dealt.

When something you need to sustain you becomes your worst enemy,
it leaves a bitter taste in your mouth.
There is no desired destination
when you're stuck on a carousel.

"Eat more food!"
"Eat less food. It's as simple as that."
Oh man, a revelation,
if only I'd met you months back,

I bet carbs are your friends as well
and you can demolish a bangers and mash.
It's a mind-set, built, mastered, perfected,
it takes time to create and even longer to crack.

If the lead in a play learnt their lines,
performed them for three months, three times a day, back-to-back,
they won't forget the mentally engrained script
after they wake up from a nap.

"You look well!"
Means I've put on weight,
means this outfit looked better on the hanger,
means I wish I had a plug to remove so I could deflate.

I always read too much into things but I can't read very well
so it comes back like a boomerang to the face.
It's a rollercoaster. I always get stuck on those,
true story, one time I was at this place,

Drayton Manor, you may know it,
at the top of Apocalypse waiting to drop, every part of my
    body braced,
except it took longer than it should have and when finally it dropped,
my stomach shifted out of place,

I guess it's not felt at home since.
The touch of sugar for a boost makes my gums wince,
no energy to workout in a culture of gym selfies and weightlifting clips,
other people's successes I like, it doesn't leave me any more convinced.

I could design a nutrition plan for someone else easily,
choosing food for my intake makes me feel queasy,
when what I eat dictates my day nothing seems complimentary,
the stress forms a lump in my throat large enough to barricade entry.

But on the days when I'm struggling to struggle,
my coffee needs a coffee and my therapist needs therapy,
on the days when I'm pushing a pull door frantically
to realise there is a button for it to open automatically,

I remind myself, if I had a bunch of seven flowers and one died,
I would throw away one, not seven,
and just because I'm focusing on designing the cover today,
I know there are pages inside still to be written.

Food and I go together like a Mento in a bottle of Coke,
the pressure bubbles up quick.
Some people have a regular public house where they go to have a drink,
I have a regular public restroom where I go to be...

If a girl vomits in a toilet
and no one is around to hear her,
did she really vomit?

Together #4

I saw in shades of black
but appeared so vibrant.

I'm scared of the dark.
I'm scared of its ability to make me compliant.
I'm scared of its comfort.
I'm scared that others will find my darkness comforting.

His Name Is...

"If you tell me his name, I have to report him."

His name is...
imagined scenarios,
it's planning her escape route,
it's staying light on her feet.
His name is walking fast,
it's blocking her path,
it's lingering in back streets.
His name is hair tucked in,
it's crossing the road,
it's taking a fake call.
His name is pulling over,
asking her for directions
instead of the man ahead who's built and 6ft 2 inches tall.
His name is following her around the store,
it's brushing past,
it's touching the small of her back.
His name is staring at her,
it's waiting for her,
it's, "look at the rack on that!"

His name is 999 already dialled,
it's stripping her of independence,
his name is keys in between her knuckles,
his name is a never-ending presence.
His name is avoiding public transport,
it's leaving the night out before it's done,
his name is dictating her skirt is too short,
it's a change of shoes that make it easier to run.
His name is hiding in the crowd,
behind buildings, bins and cars,

his name is pressed up against her,
it's using code words at the bar.
His name is continuing to ask questions
even though he hears no answer,
his name is turning innocent sentences provocative
and labelling it as 'banter'.

His name is texting when she gets home,
it's walking clear of alleyways and ditches,
his name is catcalling and dog whistles,
but we're not pussies and we're not bitches.
His name is pepper spray, it's a rape alarm,
it's impacting her mental health,
his name is triple checking a taxi number plate,
his name is her not leaving her house.

"If you tell me his name, I have to report him."

His name is...
ten years on,
his name is suffocating me,
his name is for the rest of my life,
his name is therapy.

"If you tell me his name, I have to report him."

His name is...
abuser,
his name is depression,
his name is anxiety.
His name is fear,
his name is panic,
his name is PTSD.
His name is nightmares,
it's in the dark,
it's lodged in my memory.

His name is control,
it's impossible to console,
his name is me never being free.

"If you tell me his name, I have to report him."

His name is...
rapist,
it's judgement,
it's a man phoning from victim support.
His name is men have torn me down
and I'm supposed to let them build me back up?
His name is taking me to court.
His name is behind closed doors,
it's loud noise,
it's sudden movements.
His name is driving too fast,
it's never in the past,
his name is, "Yes, but can you prove it?"

"If you tell me his name, I have to report him."

His name is...
knowing if I say it,
it's me who's more at risk.
It's keeping myself out of danger,
in turn, doing the same for him.
His name is being so short of options
it makes me physically sick.

"If you tell me his name, I have to report him."

His name is...
in safe hands.

Her name...
is never going to feel safe again.
Her name is affected,
disconnected,
neglected
and disrespected.

His name is going to haunt her.
His name is going to take her life.
His name is...
protected.

Together #5

When my world got turned upside down,
I realised, the whole time it had been the wrong way around.

Life is a joke,
if death is the punchline, we have to laugh in the face of it to keep
our feet on the ground.

We're in a dress rehearsal for a show that is going to get cancelled,
there's room for fuckups this time around.

Jordan Boyd

You waltzed in with a smirk,
we all sniggered,
I don't have a valid explanation,
perhaps because you were bigger?

Or because your hair was aglow
like a traffic light that says, "If it's clear you can go."
You were confident,
yet you didn't know

what you were getting yourself in for
with a class full of girls,
Child Development was a strange choice
but we weren't aware you were about to change our worlds.

We shouldn't have laughed
as you reeled off your unusual family tree,
but we did and you laughed with us,
we were just kids, you see.

That week, we spoke for hours.
What I'd give for those hours again.
Without hesitation you made friends with everyone,
within days they all knew your name.

Our friendship spiralled quickly
and was built on a long-lasting foundation
and bailing you out of awkward situations
at midnight at a petrol station.

If there was ever an opportune moment
to make a sexual innuendo,
you'd definitely got those covered.
Endless conversations surrounding hookers and blow.

Only you could have gotten a job
serving pints illegally at the pub,
you were a mere seventeen,
giving out free drinks and free grub.

Our car rides in the gold Daewoo,
belting Afroman as loud as you could,
pulling up next to innocent strangers
to talk to them about morning wood.

That phone call,
it hit my stomach right at the pit.
"He was in an accident
and he didn't make it."

All our worlds crumbled,
you'll never know the extent
to which you impacted all our lives
and left your Jordan-shaped indent

in our hearts,
in our minds,
on the school,
you really were one of a kind.

Walking into the exam hall,
your chair sat empty, I felt pain sear
through us as we looked around
as if you were going to appear.

The first time we saw our teachers,
the emotion made us weak,
the History teacher you perved on all year,
she broke, unable to speak.

Since that day,
I've struggled to fully express
how much I miss your ginger hair
and the way you liked to dress.

Every time I hear that song,
I can't help but feel you there as I emotionally sing along.

No matter how much time passes,
it doesn't get any easier to process
that the world has lost a human
who was destined for such greatness.

Within your short life,
you made yourself more memorable than most,
you're a connection that draws so many people together
and keeps nostalgia close.

You may now be a memory
but you are the most treasured one we keep.
Rest easy Jord and don't forget us.
Until we meet again, when I fall asleep.

~ In memory of the legend Jordan Boyd. Bro, you are so missed.

Together #6

Putting yourself first does not mean
putting yourself above someone else.

Why love yourself?
Well, it's harder to do right by someone you don't.

I'm Talking To You

I feel like you're sad.
Not all of the time.
But sad.
And that's fine.

I feel like you're angry.
Not all of the time.
But angry.
And that's fine.

I feel like you're at a loss.
Not all of the time.
But lost.
And that's fine.

I feel like you're overwhelmed.
Not all of the time.
But overwhelmed.
And that's fine.

I feel like you're hurting.
Not all of the time.
But hurt.
And that's fine.

And that's fine.
And that is fine.
Without these difficult emotions you're recognising,
you wouldn't recognise the opposite ones when they enter your life.

Scream if you have to,
cry if you need to,
stomp your feet if you want to
because you're supposed to feel what's inside of you.

Embrace every piece of you,
even the pieces that make you mad,
feel them like they're supposed to be there
rather than treating them like they're nothing but bad.

Respect their presence,
it is temporary but it is there to show you a way,
a way to discover acceptance,
a way to find a better day.

Together #7

I was told to always make my bed before leaving the house
but what if I'm not leaving my bed?
It's hard to wake up to someone you don't respect,

isn't depression a funny thing?
I wish mine would take a flying leap off a bridge,
leave me at the top.

We have to let things hit us for them to bounce back off
and "it could be worse" is a dumb response.
It's all about perspective.

Friends

I want to tell you about my friends.
One in particular a little more because today we spent a lot of
        time together,
we sat on the floor, we didn't talk,
the silence said it all.

This friend gets me,
understands that sometimes I can't do,
I just need to be,
but we have this third friend who exhibits intrusive signs
        of jealousy.

Anxiety can't keep still,
speaks too fast for me with a tendency to bring up old subjects
        carelessly.
Today, Depression and I just wanted to sit quietly,
in a darkened room sipping our tea,

feeling safe in the familiarity of melancholy company,
balancing precariously on a nine-month waiting list,
avoiding any signs of Vitamin D
as our only current form of therapy

but then Anxiety showed up which, let's face it, they always do
and they just asked questions constantly.
Depression acknowledges my reasons for avoiding things and tends
        to agree,
Anxiety questions my excuses and leaves me feeling guilty.

I've become so in touch with my friends,
they don't like it if I don't check in for a while
but being numb makes getting ready for a day you didn't plan on
     being here for
less of an arduous trial.

I am one monumental mood swing
disguised as a mammal from the wild,
using more concealer to hide my invisible scars than my
     physical ones,
with the most flawless brand I've found being My Smile.

The only thing on fleek are my inflections
and my waterproof mascara labelled with Denial,
I am a double, triple, quadruple entendre
dressed up as being versatile.

I started this journey at rock-bottom
and I know I've made headway
but the more I sweep under the rug, the more it makes for
     unsteady terrain
and I'm losing my stability again.

Today it feels like the rock at the bottom is on top of me,
I am deeper and darker than I've ever been,
finding comfort in the control of ceasing reality,
finding confusion in not wanting to live but not wanting to die and
     running out of options pretty swiftly.

Sometimes I want to keep it to myself,
I've known people to put a value of a million bucks on their two cents,
while I'm studying for my masters in my own mental health,
I won't risk copying someone else's answers to find each one was an
     uneducated guess.

But I will break in front of you,
so you know it's okay too,
I used to be the one who thought a smile spoke the truth,
I know it's possible to update a life-long view.

I wish for a world in which this can be understood
without first-hand experience and a science experiment of tablets to tend to.

I don't like the weekend, it makes those days special
when I've spent months convincing myself each day is important.
I wish days away as though having less
would lessen the urge to stay conveniently dormant.

Labels
feel like understatements.
One part of me struggles to breathe,
another reminds me I'm only panicking because I dared to be complacent.

Flash-forwards of it always being this way,
as painful as the flashbacks that cause constant anticipation,
skin sits under fingernails
to advertise my impatience.

It's a lot to happen under the roof of a day and I'm feeling beat,
I think I need to retreat, maybe just a week,
but I fear when I return
five friends will have fallen at my feet.

They've been there as solid as concrete
when my instability has reached its peak
to remind me this is something I can
and will always defeat.

When they're struggling with their direction,
I'm not comfortable taking a back seat,
I want to be their co-pilot
until their turbulence is complete.

So today, when my phone lit up
followed by that well-rehearsed beep,
I knew it was right to buckle in,
not to pass the time with sleep.

My mate was confiding in a text that they're having a rough time,
I didn't know what to suggest,
I replied including a lot of punctuation
so I had time to catch my breath,

assuring my will-power failure didn't trip their switch
and have a knock-on effect.
When the tsunami hits, we pull out our surfboards and ride the wave
    of emotion together
until our feet and solid ground reconnect.

We are clouds,
shapeshifters and drifters,
we disappear without a whimper,
we feel heavier in the winter,

we get spaced out,
our cracks showing clearly,
cast shadows over lives
whilst they watch from a distance trying to figure out what they
    can see.

Some hours, we're as blank as a new page
ready to be expressed,
carrying with us tiny pieces of heaven
waiting for them to manifest,

we swell with emotion until we burst,
raining down, causing distress
and when it's thunderous it can be frightening
but it's all part of a natural process.

We cover up the Sun
to uncover silver linings.
I won't accept an apology they didn't need to give
in a message they sent when they wanted to go into hiding.

There is no 'I' in 'team'
but there is 'tea',
so they came over, I popped the kettle on
and we worked together on surviving.

Multiple friends
living with multiple personality disorders,
living on boundaries in a parallel universe
with unparalleled lines shaping our borders,

to frame us out to be pictures of perfection
in an unforgiving exhibition of emotion hoarders,
all original
but by no means made to order.

Hung on walls,
weathered down to different hues,
built using contrasting materials,
some gruelling to get over, some simpler to break through,

built on foundations that are level
or foundations that are skewed,
built in minutes or over decades
of trying to enforce solitude.

Each wall showcasing a climb,
each climb appearing different from afar
but magnitude should not be confused
with perspective,

we shouldn't underestimate another's hurdle
when ours appears more impressive,
by adjusting our view, we can help each other to find an escape route
which is far less exhausting and far more effective.

Today, my head hurts
from banging it off my wall.
As I poured a second brew,
I considered leaning back on my friend for their support.

I wouldn't lean on a post that was too weak to hold me up,
I'd be in for a fall,
I'd look for another that could hold my weight
or stand alone as a last resort.

Today, I decided to withdraw,
keep my thoughts inside my head.
When they were ready to stand alone, they made the call,
then I climbed into my notebook, used the next page as a blanket
      and put this to bed.

Together #8

I haven't learnt how to climb walls,
I crash straight through,
use the rubble to build something new,
most likely, something for you.

Trying to build a future in a world
that is crashing down.
My lies stretch as far as "I'm fine"
before asking you and hoping you tell me the truth.

I'll tell you I'm okay
because I would give you anything you want
and you want me to be okay.
I pray, you don't lie to me the same way.

Did I?

When I cut myself free,
did I cut you open at the same time?
Did I break your heart as obliviously as he broke mine?
Did I patch myself up whilst you were still lost inside?

I remember, when the Moon told me how you make him lighter,
he had worry in his eyes,
I think he was worried I would dim your shine,
am I the reason you find it easier to cry?

Did I spend so many nights getting to know your stars
that, for you, they won't align?
Any time someone doesn't recognise you, do you think they're
    having a flashback?
Or do you know you slipped their mind?

Are you being nice to me?
Or treading on eggshells?
When someone hugs you do you question whether it's purely for you
or for them as well?

Do you avoid crowds now?
Am I the reason you check in with everyone more?
And why, when they don't reply,
you're around there knocking on their door?

When I didn't reply for days,
you drove to mine in a haze,
expecting an ambulance to interrupt your gaze,
when you found me untouched and unfazed,

you broke.
Did I break you?

When someone stares into space for too long,
do you wonder whether they have an internal war waging on?
Are you too anxious to queue?
Did you put so much faith in me, you have no faith left to put in you?

Do you twitch at night?
Did you spend so many sleepless to make sure I didn't scratch or bite
that now lying in peace doesn't sit right?
Can you sleep without leaving on a light?

Does your skin crawl?
Do you miss out on doing things you didn't question doing before?
Does your skin crawl?
Is your heartbeat louder and your breath unsure?

Does your skin crawl?
My skin still crawls,
my skin crawls at the thought of this now all being yours.
Can you not get back to how you were?

Because you've learnt too much about the world and what can occur.
When you ask someone how they are, do you ask twice
and listen more carefully to their second reply?
Do you know that people don't commit suicide, from suicide
    they die?

Did I help you to understand?
Please, tell me I helped you to understand.
Or do you wish I'd fallen out of reach
the day you stretched out your hand?

Together #9

I'm that annoying person who sees beauty in everything
but not annoying enough to tell you.

Maybe I should.
When I couldn't see it, I wasn't doing so good
and the day we stop believing our voices can make a difference
is the day they stop making a difference.

I'll put my words where my mouth is.
Until you're ready, I'll believe in you enough for the both of us.

Self-Sabotage

We've been moving cautiously for one road too long.

Let us unfasten our seatbelts and open the throttle.

We'll convene on the rocks at the foot of the cliff.

And ogle at the precipice while we split the bottle.

Stars

Don't call them scars,

call them stars.

They made it through the darkness,

show you've come so far.

Together #10

My parents raised me to see I am beautiful,
not to see my flaws.
It taught me to see that you are
and it taught me not to see yours.

I love humans,
I just don't like people.
We turned humans into people, people suck.
Supporting each other as passionately through our struggles
as we do our successes,
that's what's up.

I will put myself down to pick you up
but sometimes I'm too heavy after.
I'll tell you things knowing you don't
but wishing you had the answer.

Train

Unlike my anxiety,
the train is late.
Destination
indefinite.

Well, I'm heading to London
but there's a confined space to contemplate
before there's a destination to navigate.
If I allow future thoughts to formulate,
they'll accumulate at an alarming rate
into an elaborate reason to eradicate
what could otherwise be great.

Enabling my head to gain weight
and my anxiety to dictate my next move,
whilst my pupils dilate
until they're narrow enough to miss the train arriving at
    platform eight,
thereby, retreating to accommodate
my ability to exacerbate everything.
Leading to at least three days in which I hibernate.

Now, I know it's been there for some considerable time
but today I am convinced it's there for me.
My favourite colour sprawled out seductively in all its glory,
assuring me a lifetime guarantee, as long as I,

"Train approaching. Stand behind the yellow line."

Respect forbidden territory.

I'm boarding.
Having waited tentatively behind my yellow line,
way behind,
behind everyone else who knows their boundaries a little
    clearer than I know mine.

The doors breathe out sealing me in just in time,
along with the air,
the only air I'm allowed for the next one hundred and
    thirty-nine minutes.
The cogs begin to grind, under my feet and in my mind.

I have a seat,
a relief,
I didn't have one assigned
and this carriage is currently nurturing one-quarter of mankind.

Opposite a middle-aged guy,
casual trousers with a shirt, loosened tie,
friendly face,
smiling eyes

or suspicious,
I can't yet decide
but I didn't reserve any air either
and he and I are supposed to share the same supply.

A voice booms from my right,
"IS THIS SEAT OCCUPIED?"
He's elderly and slight,
my lips stay close to airtight for my one-word reply.

I didn't keep the conversation short for him to try harder
or to be impolite,
he hasn't realised he should preserve his breath,
I'm trying to share my foresight.

Do I have to sacrifice mine
if the pregnant lady three rows down needs me to oblige?
She's breathing for two,
my actions should coincide with health and safety guidelines.

I breathe discreetly
acknowledging it's one of my worst habits.
My desired window seat
an escape away from the on-board traffic.

The reality in passing
wreaks havoc with my panic,
how are you supposed to ground yourself
when every movement is mechanic?

A second train screeches by like a flashback screaming through
    my mind,
makes my heart and breath skip at the same time,
NO! I needed that breath, I'd only counted up to three,
each in-breath is supposed to last up to five.

Air distributes evenly
between available lungs
but I require more
after the surprise that's just been sprung.

The old fella's wasting his
on the tune he's decided to hum,
a teenager is expelling one air pocket
with every careless chew of their gum.

No one will share.
Not that I've asked.
I don't desire to conversate with smiling/suspicious eyes
    guy opposite
who has crumbs falling in his lap,

who learnt to chew in a helicopter,
each mouthful leaving my eardrums mashed,
every unconscious tap of his foot
forcing my senses into a train crash.

He's looking at me, I can feel his eyes penetrating my cheek,
he wants a chat to help time pass
but we have nothing in common
except our love of egg and cress sandwiches and our preference
    of inhaled gas.

If I turned my head any further to the window
I would ring out my oesophagus,
surely, it's obvious
there's nothing I want to discuss.

He should follow the old guy's lead,
settle down for a nap,
rather than catering to my every distaste,
provoking a respiratory system collapse.

If he doesn't stop, I'm going to
do nothing, let's be honest, except sit in discomfort and despair,
breathing politely through the involuntary caress of my every sense
assaulting me in my chair.

Imagining the power lines over-head could shock some sense
    out of me,
leaving me less aware,
as though causing torture to relieve torture
acts as some sort of repair.

"I like your hair."

My eyes dart around searching for the bullseye,
someone's inhaled too much,
I need to suss out who looks high,
my movements are becoming shaky,
I'm the one who's looking sly,
this is the third time my in-breath
has had to be re-tried.

"I like your hair."

Avoid eye contact,
just act shy,
I'm not guilty,
why is my instinct to get up, run and hide?

All I've done is comply
to make sure we all get through this ride,
my efforts have gone awry,
I'm in a line-up being identified.
Tiny sounds magnified,
air almost completely dry,
I want to speak to clarify,
if I open my mouth I'm going to cry.

"Your hair, it's nice. The first stop is in two minutes if you need to step outside."

I gaze past the piece of cress
balanced precariously on his thigh,
cautiously
find his eyes.

"I know how it feels, I'm probably not the one to give advice but count your breaths, this will pass and the air will replenish each time people alight."

Air seeped in every so often,
during the constricted travel he encouraged my breathing
    to soften.
I enquired about his mismatched choice of attire,
he explained how travelling in his full suit makes his chest feel
    on fire.

"Maybe I'm buying suits one size too small," he laughed, "but I'd rather travel comfortably at the expense of lookin' like a fool than breathe in gasps. And I'd love to be able to sleep away the journey like that," he pointed towards the elderly chap, "but my anxiety would think I was luring it into a trap."

He smiled.
I smiled back.

One hundred minutes passed
in a back and forth of deep breaths and light conversation.
He caught up with my racing heartbeat
every time he sensed its escalation.

His stop came one before mine,
he stood, looked into my eyes and spoke to my heart,
"You're going to be just fine."
Then he waved me goodbye at the window and I felt like a movie
    in black and white.

Although each breath from here took more concentration,
I took each one with a smile.

As I approached London Euston, I realised,
I didn't even ask his name.
But it turns out he has smiling eyes.
Maybe he'll remember the girl he helped on the train.

I'll remember him.
How he complimented my hair,
our shared sandwich preference
and, most of all, the kind man who shared with me his air.

Together #11

I'm so lonely
but nowhere near alone.

The kind of lonely that stops me screaming at a spider,
makes me name it, confide in it, share my home,
knowing it has no ears to absorb my pain,
catch it, set it free, wishing for me it could do the same.

Maybe it was lonely too?
Maybe it needed me today?

Tiffany

Not known him a week,
under the sheets,
knowing the same happened to me,
he starts telling me about his friend, Tiffany.

How she was abused,
mentally, physically, emotionally.
How she feels guilty
for how it's affected both her and her family.

He asks if we can write a list,
he practically insists, a list for Tiffany which consists
of reasons why it was not her fault.
A reminder, she deserves to exist.

He puts the pen in mine,
I understand,
I begin to write reasons why
it was completely out of her hands.

It was not Tiffany's fault because...

> She was coerced.
> Gas lit.
> He didn't listen when she didn't ask for it.
> She was scared.
> In denial about how bad it had become because, before it
> turned evil, she thought maybe he could be the one.
> She couldn't run, he'd chase her down before she reached
> anyone.
> She had nowhere to run, he'd isolated her from everyone.
> This was her life, the only one she had, and it was just the

way it was.
He created a dependency in him by pushing everything else away.
Rid her life of any value, her self-worth made to pay the price of his rising position day after day.
He took her love like she was in debt to him, giving nothing in return except shame.
Given liability anytime things were on the rocks, he made her take the blame for things that shouldn't be condemned.
Inflated his worth to diminish hers, grandiosity to condescend.
No respect.
Intimidated, undermined, bullied, threatened, judged with every move.
Watched her every move.
Every move he had to approve and if he disproved, oh, how she knew.
Terrified of the consequences, into a scapegoat she was made.
He played the victim, let her believe she was becoming crazed.
He remained unfazed, created confusion through his manipulative ways.
He lit the gas and turned it up as far as it would go.
Scorched perceptions of the world.
Charred the meaning of the word no.
He said mean things as if they were a joke.
Normalised unhealthy behaviour, made it appear acceptable.
When her Catherine wheel of tears spun-out, he'd insist she was making a spectacle.
He put himself on a pedestal.
Made out she was jealous of other girls.
How could she be green-eyed when the colour had drained through her cries?

He projected his fears through his lies.
Her love was weaponised.
She sacrificed herself for him like he expected her to do.
She became a shadow of herself.
When he took away the last glimpse of light, the shadow disappeared too.
Nothing was as it appeared.
The person she knew never truly existed.
He was the only person she had to turn to and so the abuse persisted, only getting more twisted if she resisted.
Broken, on the inside.
Outwardly, holding it together.
If cracks began to show he sealed them with unbearable pressure until there appeared to be no damage whatsoever.
Superficial measures.

It was not Tiffany's fault because...

He lied to everyone.
He told her he loved her each time the abuse was done.
In front of others his character was easy-going and fun.
To speak out about abuse, it takes more than being strong.
For a moment, you have to believe you are not wrong.
Believe that life will go on.
And get better.

It was not Tiffany's fault because...

She didn't want to let her family down.
He'd run her confidence and individuality into the ground.
In an effort to protect them, she'd pretend when they were around.
You wouldn't blame someone who was held under water until they drowned.
She was being suffocated.
Forced to endure pain until she was so numb the treatment

was tolerated.
His affection activated like a jukebox.
Captivated by the change of tune, she would dance along his track hoping it wouldn't end soon but she paid for this number and his moment was opportune, to reinforce hope that somewhere in there something had awoke, that things were going to change.
Moments after, silence.
Then silence turned to rage.
He set the mood with his de-human eyes and she's back to earning some small change.

It was not Tiffany's fault because...

He didn't want her, not really.
He just wanted control.
No one can be blamed for seeking love, it's literally every body's goal.
To belong. To feel whole.
This was all she knew of love and she wanted to believe in it.
She knew to make a successful relationship you have to be willing to commit.
Anytime she'd resist, he'd tighten his grip.
Forced to submit.
Abuse is never the victim's fault.
Whether child or adult, relationship or cult, abuse is never the victim's fault.

I hand him the list,
he takes it with a breath,
turns to sit facing me, he says,
"All the reasons why you, Jemima, weren't to blame and aren't to feel guilty."

With only my tattoos to keep me warm,
I felt exposed in more ways than one.

Tiffany may not be real
but her situation very much is.
It's easy to get caught up in our own point of view
rather than seeing it from someone else's.

The next time you need to,
when your trauma is causing you frustration,
try to consider what your advice to Tiffany would be,
if it was her in your situation.

Together #12

If you're sad today, that's okay,
one day you won't be again and that will be really fucking cool.
If you can't feel the Sun, please,
let it feel you.

I'll complain I'm lacking Vitamin D
but moan when the Sun is in my eyes.
When your clouds become the Sun's disguise, make shapes,
make them crazy,

crazy makes beautiful art,
pick your form and start,
if you tell me you can't, I agree,
but if you tell me you can, I will still agree.

In a world where you can be anything, be
anything.

If I was an insect, I would want to be an ant,
I want us to work together like that,
get in and explore places many don't go,
effortlessly carry weight until we can let it go.

Shakespeare

I have never understood Shakespeare
which made writing this commission about Shakespeare
    really hard.

I once told someone he was my favourite poet
because they asked
and because my mind is a graveyard
always resurrecting the past.

I sit backwards on trains to look at where I've been, contemplate
    the significance.

The truth is, his words go right over my head
and I feel small when I can't find meaning,
he makes my brain stutter,
the same line keeps repeating.

Hesitating in your mind is not comfortable
when it's an open wound, still weeping.
Hesitating in your mind is not comfortable
when it's an open wound, still healing.

I can't read someone else's story without my own story intervening.

"I understand a fury in your words/ But not the words."
Othello, act four, scene two.
We're all multi-lingual, we can scream and cry in every language
because emotion translates the truth.

He writes words in the wrong order, yes,
but when has anything ever made sense?
Like, why it took me until the age of twenty-five
to learn that sex isn't just for men.

Questions of whether he wrote his work,
dissociation is my defence,
emotions split so far apart
they created four new segments,

a personality iridescent.
Five backward trains of thought
travelling through one head,
are our words ever our own when so much has already
    been said?

It starts with something mundane,
pulls you in until you're surrounded by the inner workings of
    my brain,
his brain,
my brain,

no method,
only madness,
ink bleeds
torrential pain.

I wonder if he slept.
Have you ever tried to sleep inside a poet's brain?
Getting into bed with trauma,
disturbed by lines to be retained.

Be well
or be a poet?
The question remains.
The storytellers of our day.

Telling tragedies,
making sure it hits as close to the tragedy itself,
hearts on sleeves,
oblivion into thin air melts.

We jump down your throat
to encourage your voice to speak out,
use metaphors to condense your thoughts
down into a nutshell,

we share for you,
we write for ourselves,
if we bite our tongues
the bitterness seeps out.

I wonder how he felt
when he wrote someone's life into a line,
whether he felt like he contained the universe in his head
all of the time,

if he felt the lows from the highs
of creativity coursing through his fault lines,
have you ever tried to live
inside an artist's mind?

We're brought up with fairy tales,
leaving our lives to be defined
by false expectations of reality.
The reality is,

things don't snap back after being displaced.
Movements cause fractures cause earthquakes,
lives unhinged by seismic waves.
His slap on the wrist was a slap in the face.

"Let grief/ Convert to anger; Blunt not the heart, enrage it."
Macbeth, act four, scene three.
This world is survival of the most tolerant,
I never expected to have to grieve for my virginity.

Yet my heart will love until it runs out of beats.

"The web of our life is of a mingled yarn, good and ill together."
All's Well That Ends Well, act four, scene three.
The conflict of something that should be pleasurable causing so much pain,
mind and body in disharmony,

he won't forget it, I will always remember it,
tomorrow and tomorrow and tomorrow,
there is a difference, you see,
I don't need evil to greet him, I just wish it would stop fucking with me.

Rape is not a traumatic event,
it is a series of traumatic events from that moment on,
if it's uncomfortable to hear it,
imagine going through it

and being told you were in the wrong
and what's done is done.
Have you ever sat with an ice pack on your heart because it won't stop burning?
Life is full of lessons, why isn't he the one learning?

I'm sorry if I struggle to catch my breath,
he took it away with him and left me for death,
if he never returns, how will I get it back in my chest?
When your go-to person hurts you then, who do you go to next?

Don't mistake my emotion for weakness.
Sometimes I don't know whether to string up bunting or a tiny violin
but the poetry is my justice
in a world I am forced to share with him.

I won't give it no credit
but I will give it no power,
write it out loud,
let him become the coward.

I may not have learnt what love is
but I sure as hell know what it isn't,
it isn't control, manipulation,
being forced or imprisoned.

The only reason I still believe in love
is because of the way I am learning to love me.
If I'd read Shakespeare sooner
I would have known love is tragedy.

He caused a landslide with his disregard of boundaries,
crashing down with the gravity of his activity
and yet I've spent my life saying sorry
to those who caught the aftershocks, making sure they don't hit
    the rocks.

I'm not good enough.
Someone else got to decide that I never would be
and this was supposed to be about Shakespeare
but I made it about me.

He taught us to speak about tragedy.
The biggest tragedy being that we don't understand each other
and that we don't try.
Not to be dramatic but misunderstanding makes people die.

Maybe we were both trying to re-write the times,
find reason through our rhymes.
I thought it was Shakespeare's fault I turned a blind eye
but the responsibility was mine,

we only listen when it applies
but we have to open up our minds and discuss to save lives,
we can't assume things don't concern us,
different doesn't mean dangerous

and our cells renew every seven to ten years, so my skin has never
    felt his touch.

We don't know it all
because rooms carry on when we leave them.
When the shit hits the fan, so do everyone's true colours,
where are you on the spectrum?

Together #13

How do our minds create such beauty
yet cause such chaos?
I have thousands of ideas
but thousands end up lost,

I am a flake.
I fall,
cling to others who have fallen until we're warm
then run away,

I don't do confrontation.
If I argue I am convinced I'm right,
it hurts me to fight,
I've been fighting myself every night for the past five years.

It's taught me to live every day like
it's a new day.
My dreams keep me awake
in this nightmare.

I have no plan,
let alone a plan B
but I will make you
believe in me.

You are a fact,
believe in yourself.
It's easier to get others to believe in something
you already believe in,

I don't want to smile if I'm not the reason
and if it doesn't reach my eyes
I will figure out the reasons,
breathe in.

Let it go.

Communication Is Sexy And Consent Is Compulsory

No means no.
Silence means no.
Sometimes no gets suffocated under the weight of an oversized ego
that needs to learn to take a no

so no can be the safeword it always should have been.
Forget pineapple, red or orange,
there has to be power in "No." "Stop."
"GET OFF ME!"

I'm going to tell you a not-so-secret,
communication is unbelievably sexy.
Speak to them directly,
avoid a situation getting sketchy,

make sure they're ready,
communication is sexy.
And consent is compulsory.
You ready?

Being of age isn't approval,
a smile isn't authorisation,
a smile can be from nervousness as easily as flirtation,
communicate before you give in to temptation.

Being drunk is no excuse,
that's not up for negotiation,
what your mates think is irrelevant,
don't let that fuel irritation,

be patient,
don't ignore hesitation,
make sure your intentions are good
and don't get lost in validation.

If what was worn was an invitation,
rape on nudist beaches
would be an uncontrollable situation.
Clothes can't give consent.

Consent won't be found through manipulation,
gyration, sedation, penetration or ejaculation
but through communication,
have the conversation.

He asked for consent
but he didn't listen to my answer.
Asking isn't enough, their answer
dictates what you do or don't do after.

He stopped trying to turn me on.
Instead, he turned on me.
Now he's a rapist and that's a label that sticks
forever, I guarantee.

Consent is free.
Rape is not.
Rape comes
at extortionate costs.

Being desperate for a shag or being a lad
isn't an excuse for being forceful,
it won't stand up in a court of law,
it doesn't matter if you're remorseful.

You don't put the *penis* into *hap-penis*,
no, this isn't just aimed at men,
the capability is anyone's,
whether he or she or them, there is no exception.

We are in this life together, we should be each other's protection.

"We don't have to do this"
is the most seductive thing anyone can say to me.
If I had a quid for every time someone has,
I'd have like two quid.

It isn't enough,
it costs nothing to talk about stuff
but rape,
rape comes at extortionate costs.

Communication is erotic,
let's make sure it isn't lost,
"Do you want to do this?"
"Is this okay?"

Forget Fifty Shades of Grey,
let's try fifty ways to make them feel safe.
Communication is sensual,
not to mention essential foreplay.

If you get into it and they change their mind,
no and *stop* still hold the same power
so pull away, get off.
Stop.

See past what you want.
Tell them it's okay,
encourage them to communicate,
reassure them they're safe.

They don't have to say what you want to hear,
they get to say what they need to say,
make them feel that way,
ask if they want to continue or not, communication is hot.

They get to choose how their body is used,
give them that choice instead of giving them trust issues.
Don't put the 'tit' into attitude and get in a mood
just because they refused,

even if you're confused, they are excused.
Their no isn't a reflection on your performance,
most of the time.
It isn't all about you.

If you've had consensual sex before,
that doesn't mean they'll want more,
you know what you need to ask for before you explore,
make sure they're sure.

Make sure you're sure they're sure.

If earlier they said yes and now they don't want to,
you don't have consent,
it's not up for debate,
you don't have an argument,

I don't care if you're discontent,
let's prevent an offence,
you scrambling for a defence
because your satisfaction

came at their expense,
if you don't have consent
nothing goes ahead.
It's common sense.

If you have to talk them into it,
it shouldn't be happening.
The fact I'm even writing this
is baffling

but people are being raped
and their lives are unravelling,
leaving years ahead of battling
to repair the damages, it's maddening.

Let's make communication more appealing
to avoid unnecessary lifetimes of healing
and dealing with feeling
like our bodies are concealing

internal bleeding
from the wound that keeps reopening
and the nightmares that keep repeating in our minds.
Peace is hard to find.

I don't want this life
for another of mankind,
the bottom line
is consent is compulsory.

Lines get blurred and lines get crossed,
read them carefully
and in between where silence sits,
make sure communication isn't lost.

Communication is hot.
Consent is legal.
No consent is rape.
A crime.

You'll do the time but so will they,
to an extent you can't even comprehend, it won't ever go away.
We pretend we're on the mend when it affects us every day,
no one deserves this kind of pain.

Don't be a criminal,
it's easy.
Communication is unbelievably sexy.
And consent is compulsory.

Together #14

I've learnt not to say sorry for things that are out of my control
but I am sorry.

I'm sorry if my mental illness is an inconvenience for you
but I can guarantee it is more of an inconvenience for me,
I want to be what you want but I have to be what I need.

Defining Moment

They say, "It doesn't define you, you know."

My neck hangs like bluebells,
the colour of my mood rings out, the blues,
instrumental in the many walks
when depression obscures the view.

Forget-me-not flashbacks,
stinging nettle skin,
soothed by a bitter dock
sapping life from within.

Daisy chains dress up the way
his weight still keeps me down,
I want to go out but his face in the clouds,
senses implode when the world resounds.

My buttercups don't reflect yellow
because butter is fat
and I can't be
because he liked me like that.

Took away my favourite colour
when he took away the Sun,
a depression that's jealous of yours
if it dares to rise in skies of fun.

I'm a honeybee,
if I wound you once it's death to me.
My thoughts are puffball dandelions,
carried away so easily.

Tornado memories
leave me shaking like a leaf.
I am mud. Dirty.
Still scrubbing myself clean.

Yet they say, "It doesn't define you, you know."

Character re-cast
with a wardrobe fit for formication,
I take my coat from the hook I'm on,
keeps me from reaching my foundation.

Take my skin crawls on long walks,
bridge railings not to be approached.
His temper left inside of me,
a temper not to be provoked.

I'm a lot for me to handle,
if only some of me could be preserved
and drip-fed in small doses
as I become ready for the reserves.

Only smile at the mirror when I look familiar,
identities people keep examining,
no one respects my new-build boundaries,
the next thing I know I'm panicking.

No bad hair days, just bad head days
when my tears fall like they're trying to give him praise,
lost my job and pursued my mental state,
went through more pain to prove I'm not insane.
There are those that exploit me for their own gain,
can't let me down because expectations were erased,
don't trust the ones by who I was cared and raised,
as someone I looked up to, he once filled that space.
I'm an explosive with potential to devastate,

I won't detonate until I'm far enough away,
a monu-mental illness to which many can't relate,
tea, two sugars tastes the same as a full plate.
Don't have a comfort zone, even on Sundays,
only time I dance is to ground when my head strays,
I live for the clarity that comes after I awake,
I'll keep waking even though my comfort is at stake.
Keep a towel by my side as a barricade,
or perhaps to clean up more of the mess he made,
if I'm going to cross you I will look both ways,
if you hit me I'll find strength in the pain.
Got more conviction than a court of magistrates,
I'm afraid to say the verdict didn't validate
but no conviction gave me more to educate,
no conviction gave me more to set the record straight.

So when they say it doesn't define me,
it makes me feel betrayed,
if to define is to describe the nature of,
my garden doesn't grow the same,
if to define is to establish the character of,
I'm unrecognisable except my name,
if to define is to mark out the boundaries of,
step back and respect my space,
if to define is to give the meaning of,
the moral of my story has been replaced.

From being fifteen with the world at my feet,
believing that people were kind,
to being the person I needed when I was sixteen,
looking fear in the eye and making it hide.

The dream was to have kids of my own
one day, to be somebody's wife.
Now the dream is to keep waking up from them,
to make sure he doesn't take more of my life.

When they say it doesn't define me,
it's more for them than me,
they feel uncomfortable that they can't fix
the problem that they see

but if they take away the problem,
I'm still left with its effects,
no trauma but post-trauma disorder,
responses to non-existent events.

I don't want to only accept
a future version of me that may never come to be
and if they're looking for the person I used to be,
they don't deserve this me.

I can't remember her,
only the events that made her leave,
let me honour the meaning,
allow me endless time to grieve.

The force of this is real,
you can't disprove gravity.
When I say that it defines me,
I don't say it in agony,

I don't know who I am without the memories
but with them, I'm resilient and I'm bold,
this world needs me,
not a version that's trying to fit the image society has sold.

Don't get me wrong, he didn't make me strong,
that was me,
but I'd like to thank him for the lives I can change by him
    ruining mine
because *that* is more powerful than an apology.

Maybe I see his face in the clouds
but a cloud is part of something much bigger,
when the clouds disappear,
the bigger picture stays here.

I don't have to find the positives in it,
I have to find the power,
when they say it doesn't define me,
it reminds me not to cower.

They mean well
but its meaning brings me tranquillity.
If every moment is a gift, I'll accept the worst ones
and use them to the best of my ability.

When they say it doesn't define me,
they undermine the position I'm in.
A defining moment is being urged to make a pivotal decision
and every day since I've had to decide to keep living.

So, to who it may concern,
it's not yours to take away,
you can stand with me until the clouds disperse
but the weather isn't yours to change,

you can be a part of the bigger picture
but you can't return the gifts he gave.
You can't say it doesn't define me
when it explains who I became.

Together #15

I have a brain and I don't know how to use it
but it outsmarts me every day.
I fall asleep to the sound of a vacuum,
every piece of rubbish from the day being taken away.

If my appointment is in three hours
I'll leave approximately fifteen minutes ago to accommodate
my anxiety.
If you say it's good to see me happy
my depression will assert its authority.

I'm too much, get sick of me.
I'm hard on myself,
not because I want to beat you,
because I want to beat me.

Pursue your dreams
with the same confidence you belt out your favourite tune in
the car.
You take up such a small one
but you play such a big part.

Dust

You were created in this universe
and you want to fit in?
Brewed in the heart of an explosion.
Stardust.

A potential five hundred million planets capable of supporting life
and we can't all support each other on one.
A single quality (and I do mean quality) receives hate
when 99.9% of species are already gone.

You are a black body.
A star.
Absorbing all radiant energy,
emitting much more by far.

They believe they are the Sun,
which is to say, you are bigger and brighter.
The human eye factors in surrounding colours so the appearance
    is whiter
but the Sun is a green star. A jealous ball of raging fire.

Your light breaks through turbulent atmosphere
illuminating the way for others,
the twinkle in your eye reveals every deflection
causing a change of intensity in your colours.

They move like the billions of lifeforms on their skin
feast on champagne and caviar,
swim in oceans accommodating two hundred thousand different
    viruses
but won't gaze upon the beauty that you are.

They're scared.

Scared they're going to catch on,
catch themselves viewing rainbows in black and white.
Supernovas brought elements essential for survival
and you are essential for this world to get survival right.

If someone looks at you like they want to fix you,
they will fall through the cracks.
Not all star systems are binary and the cosmos exists naturally,
it does not have to apologise for the way it acts.

Are you a galaxy?
With a black hole at the centre of you?
Black holes are very, very cold
but galaxies will not be consumed.

Gravitational attraction pulls in matter,
this force works to ground you,
try to keep a stable orbit
until this force of nature is through.

One hundred and forty billion (or so) galaxies,
you're not alone in this gloom
and you're about to be on fire
because when a flame burns at its hottest, it appears blue.

13.8 billion years old,
getting more interesting by the day,
your age adds to your wonder,
it doesn't take your worth away

A teaspoon of neutron star
weighs about a billion tonnes
and your weight or size
doesn't dictate your levels of attraction.

More than twenty-four time zones
means you and your anxiety made it on time,
when you look into the starry sky you're looking deep into the past
so your punctuality after sunset is sublime.

Outer space is open to interpretation
and your silence is of tremendous value.
Needing spectacles doesn't make you a spectacle
when 95% of the universe is out of view.

I guess what I'm trying to say is, survival on Earth is unnecessarily difficult
and lives are so good at ruining lives
but if we judge those who judge us, we resolve nothing.
Accepting ourselves is how we survive.

You see, you stand out against the backdrop of this universe
and almost all ordinary matter is empty space.
If someone struck a match on the Moon, astronomers could spot the flame,
by which I mean, the right people will see you and your qualities will be embraced.

Finding flaws in someone else doesn't make our own less visible,
throwing shade won't change the shade of someone's skin,
if you touch two pieces of the same type of metal together in the vacuum of space,
they will fuse. Rainbows have always created a happiness within.

The static of a retro television
displays the Big Bang afterglow,
we won't always have the correct channel of thought
but the reason is bigger than we know.

Yes, the Sun rages but it can still bring warmth and light
and space has enough space for us all to progress.
At the bare bones of it we are all the same
and if we are all simply dust, isn't it time we clean up our mess?

Together #16

Life is a life-or-death situation.

I want you to know,
you don't have to play the cards you've been dealt.

Rip up the pack,
create confetti
and celebrate love for yourself.

Road To Anywhere

I'm starting out on a new road.
It's an open one.
A road to acceptance that emphasises
he didn't make me what I've become.

This road doesn't wind,
it has no wrong turns,
it has no unexpected bends,
it has only learning curves.

I know because this road is manmade
and that man, is me.
My road doesn't have an end,
my road is everything I wish it to be.

Beside my road there runs a stream
that maintains a gentle flow,
a problem finished with will be placed on the ripples
and carried away as the breeze will blow.

The trees with leaves of greens and orange
provide the air for calming breaths,
Jasmine Cottage bestows a feeling of warmth,
forget-me-nots scour the length and breadth.

There is no light at the end of the tunnel
because the Sun never ceases to shine,
no speed limit demanding expectations,
'Road to Anywhere' is the only sign.

One day, there will stand a hitchhiker
at the side of my road,
I know that hitchhiker will be him
but I won't ask for him to go.

I'll look briefly in his direction and smile,
a smile radiating peace and bliss.
He can stay on my road now,
it's been far too long that I've been on his.

He is not responsible for my vices,
not my virtues, nor my woes,
no, no, no that's giving him far too much credit,
an inconvenience is as far as it goes.

I won't stop to give him a ride,
I'll watch as many more pass him by.
That will be the last I watch of him,
from then on, he can watch me fly.

Together #17

Long story long, you're alright,
however you are.
Roses are red, yellow, white, pink,
how deceptive it is to put a limit on how we think.

The sight of someone feeling like they have to wear a disguise
makes me want to ring out my eyes.
If you need to, take a minute,
a day, a week, a month but please, not your life.

Dear Men

Dear men,
we wanna see you cry,
let the emotion overflow
and bring tears to your eyes,
let them stream.
Scream,
vexation is valid,
we know your hearts burn too,
don't pretend you're rock solid,
you're not a rock,
we don't expect you to be,
doesn't mean you can't be ours when we need somewhere to lean
but you're human
and you deserve to feel seen
even when your role is not to be the hero on the screen.
I've seen
men bottle it up until it brings them to their knees
because double standards set by society
say that women are warmth
and men's emotions must freeze.
It's time to thaw.
Let expectations cease.

Stereotypes exist
because we're scared of complexity,
we simplify out of fear
at the expense of identity,

you're man not machine,
yes, your brain functions chemically
but you're not a scientist
concocting your own body's chemistry.

Fuck stereotypes,
you don't have to dry your eyes before you speak to me.

My phone's facial recognition doesn't see me if I'm crying,
see, we shouldn't be machines because they're guilty of denying
access to areas on which we are relying,
for us to see it's you, you don't have to be smiling.

We're taught seeing is believing
so your depression is hiding,
behind gritted teeth
the anxiety is grinding,

if it costs your mental health,
then baby, you ain't buying
because men keep on paying
and men keep on dying.

This world doesn't deserve you
but you do.

Why do we discard broken records
when we should be holding them together?
Long enough to hear them out,
to turn the tables on conjectures,

to scratch the surface of what's needed
to heal from the pressure,
to rebalance, avoid sticking
and hear their song play out forever.

If you feel the same today
as the last time I asked,
tell me again and again and again,
don't pretend it's passed.

Depression is a very natural response to life,
those who contain so much darkness exude so much light,
when you run in polar circles and you live in polar night,
you want to protect others from living with that fight.

Don't say what you think people want to hear,
say what you need to say,
your free time and availability are not the same,
it's okay if you can't today,

what you don't do today isn't a detriment to you,
it's an opportunity for the future to embrace,
do what's right for you rather than what's expected
and remember, persistence over pace.

Life is not too short, it is long and hard,
you have time to feel this out,
it's hard to figure out your own brain with your own brain,
reach out, let another one help.

I'm not saying give up,
I'm saying give in,
breakdown to breakthrough,
don't let the double standard win.

Asking for help does not show weakness,
it shows you're ready to build your strength,
you're endangered, there's only one of you left,
protect you at any lengths.

I know so many people who can't remember a life before
    depression,
that doesn't mean there isn't a life with depression
and that doesn't mean there isn't a life after depression.
You aren't supposed to know how to live with it but acceptance is
    key to progression.

When you're so tired you consider throwing yourself down the stairs
to save the effort of walking,
when you want to follow your heart but it's broken into pieces,
when your whole life hurts, start talking.

If someone judges you,
it says more about them than it does about you,
don't apologise for a conclusion
someone else jumps to.

If they think you're too much,
they can settle for less elsewhere
but your heart is vital and breakable
so please, handle with care.

Future-you is so proud of you for getting through this,
for finding opportunity in crisis,
keep goin'.

In this life, you're up against you,
you know what that means?
It means you win.

Dear men,
we wanna see you cry.
When your whole life hurts
let it fall from your eyes,
let it out.
Shout,
make room for new feelings,
you're stronger than you've been,
you'll get stronger from here,
pain has meaning,
meaning demands to be seen,
it doesn't want to get lost so it really makes a scene,
act it out,

let the meaning take the lead,
let it guide to what you need,
let yourself pay heed.
I've seen
men bottle it up until it brings them to their knees
because double standards set by society,
say that women are warmth
and men's emotions must freeze.
It's time to thaw.
Let expectations cease.

Together #18

I believe our paths, yours and mine,
they were meant to cross,

we just had some learning curves to navigate along the way,
maybe ended up a little bit lost

but this was worth living for
and of moments like this, there will be more.

Kintsugi

If you think I'm a mug,

drop me.

Like Kintsugi,

I'll piece myself back together with gold,

keep the repair as an important part of my history.

Bravery

We're told kindness doesn't cost us anything

but that isn't true, is it?

People take advantage of kindness all the time

so kindness can come at a cost.

Being kind is an act of bravery.

Be brave.

Together #19

There's an 'ours' in 'yours'
so let's share.
Our ears keep growing to remind us to keep listening,
to be sure when someone needs to feel heard
the means is there.

Let's write as though no one is ever going to hear it
and share it as though everyone should.
Something you say today could help someone else
to feel far more understood.

Every Woman Who's Ever Been Abused Should Get To Spend The Night With You (To Clarify, I Don't Want Them To)

Every woman who's ever been abused should get to spend the night
  with you.
(To clarify, I don't want them to.)

For every man who took a step too close,
you take a step back,
for every time he ignored a no,
you double-check to counteract,

listen to my words of consent,
then let my body interact,
make sure it agrees with me
because it works a little differently.

You hug me for me, not for you,
to avoid imposition,
green lights are for those
who wait patiently for permission.

You listen, I know you listen,
you remember everybody's names,
I haven't put a name to a face
since his became a source of pain.

When you say my name,
it's wrapped safely around your tongue,
nothing forcing me to respond,
when we kiss, I don't taste the past anymore but I'm not afraid to
  feel young.

When I pull away, you stay,
don't get closer,
bring our bodies together with your timing,
an experienced composer,

let me analyse the evidence of your body,
full disclosure,
so there's no way you can become him,
reassuring my composure.

"Remember where you are,
remember who you're with,
put your hand on my chest
and listen to me breathe,
it's just you and me.
Let's breathe.
It's okay to have a weep,
crying doesn't make you weak,
if you're tired from all the fighting we can rest and go to sleep,
just breathe."

I'm drunk on your questions,
"Am I doing too much?"
Intoxicated with lust,
sobered up by trust.

"We can adjust,
there's no rush,
stopping isn't a fuss,
we can discuss
what you need
to feel safe with my touch
and if it's all too much
don't just push through,
I'm here for you."

I seek validation in sex,
a side effect of the trauma,
you seek validation your actions are correct,
me the teacher, you the performer.

Thank me for granting access to my body,
remind me it's a place of worship,
that only people who believe in me can enter,
stay as long as their faith doesn't slip.

This place
is sacred.

No hero complex,
or perhaps, an awareness that all men have one,
an awareness that you need to rein it in
because, "Baby, you are not broken."

I don't need to be fixed,
my symphony
is a remix
and you're putting your beat to it.

Every woman who's ever been abused should get to spend the
    night with you.
(To clarify, I don't want them to.)

You follow me into the flashbacks
to bring me back in a flash,
encourage me to stay
but wait until I get back.

Tracing the lines on your hands,
I'm seeing your future while you're witnessing my past,
your hands become a raft,
a lifeboat between me and his wrath.

You sit with me in the past,
we re-write the narrative until his intentions are dashed,
you treat me like nothing has happened once it's passed,
no questions asked. Just,

"I know you don't feel it
but I want you to know you're safe.
I know you don't think it
but I need you to know you're doing great."

I say I'm sorry I am this way,
you tell me you're not,
you're sorry about the trauma,
not for the way my body survives the scars it's got.

You kiss my stretchmarks
as though they show how far I've stretched myself for people,
kiss the imprints of my bra
because support shouldn't leave a dent to be healed,

I don't hold my stomach in
because I don't have to shrink myself to fit your ideal,
I'm a whole five courses with a coffee and a mint
not just a main meal.

Hold me like I'm yours,
treat me like I'm mine.
We take
my time.

You see the parts I've tried to disguise
my whole life,
the thighs I've tried to reduce in size
my whole life,

the parts I give the least attention to,
you pick them first,
my worst your most desired,
societal expectations in reverse

but you don't take,
you share me with me
because teamwork makes the dream
a reality.

I say, "You drive me crazy."
You say, "See, crazy can be a good thing."
Knowing I've used it to my detriment too many times,
acknowledging others have struck me with its sting.

I scream, "My God!"
And you're making an atheist believe.
I imagine if God did make you, she took a day off,
knew she'd peaked.

Maybe we'll keep this going
until the passion on one side outweighs the other,
until my thighs loosen their grip
and we replace the covers

or perhaps they'll tighten,
revealing more than lovers.
Regardless, a person should know when they change something
so powerfully for another,

so this is my message to you
for empowering me to rediscover a part of me that was left to suffer,
for realising one wrong move removes progress,
for understanding I can't simply just recover.

Every woman who's ever been abused should get to spend the night with you.
(To clarify, I don't want them to.)

To clarify, I don't want them to.

Together #20

If your game face is flawless, that worries me.
It doesn't need to be.

I've seen things with eyes open that some couldn't conjure up with theirs shut,
now they're there every time mine close, but
what if, let's just say, everything is going to be okay again one day?
Shouldn't we be here for that?

Let's be here for that.
Together.

This Is Not A Motivational Speech

You are ready.
What for?
You tell me,
you see...

Or maybe you don't.
Has the light gone out?
The one that was your guide,
that gave you direction with every stride.

Now it's black,
pitch black.
You can't see ahead,
maybe you can't even see back.

Do you feel opaque
like no one can see inside
but terrified to be transparent
with nowhere left to hide?

All your life
you've given pieces of you away,
handed them out to others
to help to brighten their day.

Then, in a moment, it hits you,
you're empty yourself.
It's time to put back the pieces you're missing,
show yourself the love you've shown to everybody else.

'But he...'
'But she...'
'But they...'
Stop. Bring it back to you today.

•

I remember being surrounded by everything I needed to live
    comfortably,
except the thoughts of a level head.
I still battle with my brain every morning to get up,
battle all over again at night to go to bed.

Some days it's still difficult to go out
even though the air is easier to breathe outside.
When I stopped running from my pain, I realised,
to move forward, my pain and I needed to collide.

I used to have a lion in my heart,
suddenly, I was allergic to cats.
I'd sleep through alarms I didn't remember to set,
brush my teeth with toothpaste and tears, curled up on the bathmat.

I'd indicate as though I was about to make a right turn,
then remember I was disorientated,
how do you go after your dreams
when your nightmares leave you tormented?

The constant conflict of no energy to do things
but wanting things done,
people stopped expecting from me,
I had no brightness left to bring to anyone.

Can you imagine if God said,
"Let there be light!"
and there wasn't?
Embarrassing, right?

Wrong.
If something doesn't connect,
we look for another solution
until the current is flowing strong.

•

When a wall goes up,
it doesn't always mean get ready to climb,
it can mean stop. Recharge your strength, then break it down,
use the debris to build something versatile that will withstand time.

Sometimes we need to shut down to update and re-boot,
a detour can end up being the more scenic route,
it's okay to say, "That sounds like an offer I can refuse",
someone else's opinion of you changes nothing, whether you
      entertain it you get to choose.

Every path that crosses ours
isn't supposed to be a diversion,
if we take a wrong turn
what's to say it won't develop into an exciting excursion?

If it feels good, do it. If it doesn't, don't.
If you don't know, wait.
Don't ask questions you don't want to know the answers to,
you wouldn't pile foods you don't like the taste of onto your already
      full-up plate.

You have as much right to be here as the person next to you,
no more, no less, the same.
You're not entitled to all things great but you are worthy of them,
if they come your way they're allowed to be claimed.

There are no expectations in this world, only experiments,
your mistakes don't define you, they refine you.
You can say, "Take me as I am or leave me where I am",
surrounding yourself with acceptance will help to see you through.

•

Sometimes your best loved teacup wears a hairline crack,
your best loved shoes cause you to slip,
your best loved cutlery can bend out of its original shape,
your best loved pillow can go flat from never being flipped.

Your favourite TV show probably contains a break,
your favourite book will become worn,
your favourite biscuit might crumble between your grasp,
your favourite t-shirt likely ends up torn.

Your favourite pen can inconveniently run out,
your favoured season experiments with change,
your chosen outdoor spot may have to withstand a storm,
sometimes your beloved pet can act somewhat strange.

Who says damaged isn't beautiful?
Who says broken isn't divine?
Who says the crooked edge of your battered heart doesn't fit
    exquisitely against the crooked edge of mine?
Who says your imperfections denote you can't be someone's best
    loved find?

•

As the Sun goes down, the tide comes in
and the wave of emotion makes it harder to breathe,
as the tide goes out and the Sun rises,
we have to try to follow its lead.

If you were about to swim deeper,
you would take a longer breath,
if you're diving down into your emotions,
expect to breathe deeper as you explore your depths.

Trust yourself, even if you can't trust anybody else.

Anytime we don't do something
we told ourselves we would,
we lose a little trust
and it gets harder to listen to ourselves when we really know
    we should.

So, dream big
but keep goals attainable,
if your goal today is to get out of bed and you do it,
trust in yourself will build towards something sustainable.

Side note: I am really fucking proud of you.

We're all striving to be butterflies
but caterpillars are beautiful too
and we have to digest everything about ourselves
before we can breakthrough.

Don't focus on what someone else is capable of,
it's okay if they're influential
but don't crave their attributes,
start falling in love with your own potential.

What if the grass is greener on the other side because it's artificial?
Surely natural growth is more beneficial?

Stack up your knock backs and climb on them,
put a negative experience to work for you,
if the universe can build up from nothing and you're a part of it,
you can too.

•

I'm not out of the woods yet
but I'm becoming grateful for the opportunity to explore
which means the light is seeping through the trees
because I can see my surroundings more and more.

I love trees. Roots as strong as my own,
growth I aspire to hone
and don't they weaken from the inside too?
I'm hanging on like a leaf but it won't be easy to tear me down.

•

You have to lose control to learn how to gain it.
Don't underestimate your strength of mind,
the mind that as a child kept you looking for solutions
even if it took up all of your time.

Usually what we think of our own ability
overshadows our actual ability.
You're not going to find yourself once,
life is a cycle to make re-adjustment a possibility.

This is a thing that you get through, let's treat it that way,
go at your own rate.
Being selfish can be necessary and you are necessary,

and *you* are worth the wait.

This is not your life,
this is your life so far.
You don't need to question whether you're worth living for,
I promise you, you are.

You

Your greatest strength is that you are you.

No one else will ever be you.

No one will ever be able to take you from you.

Therefore, you will always have strength in you.

Before I go, I want to tell you a very quick story.

When I went through sexual trauma and an attempted kidnapping at the age of sixteen, I wrote a diary throughout and afterwards. Nine years later, I found that diary. I decided I wanted to burn it, I guess I thought that I could burn his memory out of my life. This wasn't the case, of course. It took a lot more than burning a diary to get to where I am today. However, I did burn it.

My friend (in the green t-shirt) and I went to the local park one night, we took the diary and a lighter and sat on the gravel car park in the dark. We tried to light the paper but it was so windy, getting it to catch alight took ages. When it finally did, it would blow out again. The fucker just would not burn! We persisted. We tried so persistently that the lighter began to run out of fluid. And if this wasn't a metaphor for how fucking difficult it would be to remove the memory of my abuser from my life, I don't know what it was.

It did burn, eventually. We burned the whole thing to ash and it felt good. We laid down on the gravel, held hands, looked up at the starry night sky and fell silent.

It was a small victory and only the start of much more hard work towards an easier, more comfortable life.

But it did get easier.
And it did get more comfortable.

Hang in there and never stop trying to light that shit up!!

Jemima introduces...

James Scott-Howes

Leicester based poet James Scott-Howes has inspired me since my early days on the poetry scene. This absolute powerhouse of spoken word keeps me on my toes, striving to match his incredible level of performance, especially since collaborating with him in 2022 with a piece we call 'Listen To His Name'. Writing on important subjects, including men's mental health and a man's perspective on the way women are treated within society, James isn't afraid to face social issues, inequalities and injustices head on. He blows audiences into the stratosphere with his impact, bringing them back down to Earth with a new outlook.

I'm stoked for future collabs. Until then, this is his poem.

A Hill I Won't Die On

There is no place in this world for sensitive men.
Unless you manage to leverage it into poems, paintings or songs, movies, slo-mo motion cap, photos and drawings that others can use as a lens to view themselves through.
Why do you think so many songs vividly paint heart breaks? Because no one wants to know a man's sadness unless there's a catchy melody attached to it.
Tough or timid, placid or livid, open or closed, open means open to mockery, so we remain closed.

How many men live rigid in cognitive dissonance?
Stiff lips and slight eyes no disguise for listlessness.
Slyly eyeing high rise heights granite in skyline, wondering what it might be like to bow out with a swan dive rather than say

'I can't do this anymore'.

When the shame weighs so greatly upon our minds, we'd rather open our skulls than our mouths to excise what's inside, something is wrong.
Nothing's wrong with us, it's with the way we're brought up.
Men can't even be friends without snickering indignity, have to be circumspect with any kind of connection, laugh too hard, find him interesting, left alone there's no chance, how long is it until someone pipes up with

'Bromance'. Calm down it's only a joke, you take everything too far.
It's a joke, like most men's feelings are.

But they aren't.

How we cope with what we feel entirely defines whether we're perceived to be real in our own and other's eyes, but I'm a man and

I cry, all the time.

I cry when I'm sad, gazing out of a window distractedly and when I'm overly happy, my eyes prickle when I reminisce, 2001 Emo classics in shuffle thrown up by a playlist, when I realised what was about to happen to Lenny, I had to take a break, because I couldn't see the page, last chapter finally finished, then when I sat in silence eyes finally dry, thought hits and I begin again when I realise that George only did what he did to be a friend.

I am real despite my overwhelm
I am real when asking for help
I am real despite being told otherwise
I am more real for having cried.
Long ago, I decided that I would not die on a hill that someone else defined.
So you can keep your definition of being a real man and I shall live and die by mine.

Instagram: @jamesscotthowes

Jemima introduces...

Claire Tedstone

I'll never forget the first time I saw Claire Tedstone perform at Leamington Poetry Festival. It was the first time she'd ever performed poetry and it wasn't going to be the last. The following year, she headlined the event alongside me. Her story is one people want to hear more of and she was destined to tell it. She has had audiences in the palms of her hands ever since, holding them tenderly but in no way holding back. Claire may see the world in different colours to you but let her paint her picture and I know you'll wish you could see it her way too. I needed to hear her poetry, I have no doubt so many more do. So, this is her poem.

Metaphormosis

My metamorphosis in metaphor

A butterfly in chains -
she remains -
until love breaks apart
and unlocks the heart
consumed with darkness
in which she is held captive.

A butterfly set free -
she sees -
a heart
broken apart
yet full of light.
She is drawn within
where she basks in the glow,
before once more taking flight.

I'm actually, best friends with a butterfly.

Some see only her beauty
and the way she flies free -
fluttering from flower to flower,
sipping sweetness hour after hour.

But they do not know the depths of her.
Could never comprehend
the creation of my friend.

They do not understand her history.
Did not see
the way she
crawled along the ground,
bound to the earth -
biting through bitterness.

They could never guess
how her voracious appetite
would lead her to consume all that was in sight.

Not now they see her here -
light and in flight.

They did not see her shed her skin
and become herself over and over again.

I wonder if she felt any pain,
that last time she shed her skin
and felt the core of her being begin to harden.

Did she feel herself dissolve in the darkness?
Breaking down alone, unnoticed,
as life continued around her in the garden.

I wonder if she knew
that she was being changed.
Parts rearranged
into something strange and new.

Or did she feel like she was dying?
Like the darkness cocooning her was the end,
with no knowledge she would soon be flying.

I wonder what it was like for you my friend.

You see, I too was once caterpillar.
Went through a matter similar to you -
a metamorphosis now familiar to you.

And I felt it all.
Every ounce of it.

The way the world burned.
My rawness -
as I turned
inside out,
emerging from a body
I no longer recognised.

My surprise -
as my once soft self
began to harden to the world.

The way my insides
melted like molten lava,
and the times I thought I'd rather
die than feel this liquid fire.

My screams -
and how nobody could hear me.
I had no body anymore.
Just the deafening, silent screams of
my soul.

My whole existence was excruciating
and I begged for it to end.

The growth of unfamiliar parts
in unfamiliar places
and how it felt like I couldn't breathe
as my space
grew too small.
The walls
of my own self
no longer able to contain
what I had become.

I felt it all.

And it was all triggered by –

him.

The ghost of him haunts me.

Unfamiliar places
we'd never been,
I could have sworn I'd just seen –

him.

Standing there
and then not.
Hair
in a top knot.

A flush of fear.
        A hint of hope.
Flames rising inside.
        Burning heart and racing mind.
Burning mind and racing heart.

I'm torn apart.

Like sunlight hitting a raindrop,
my sense of self refracts -
splits into a spectrum -
and she reacts,
and I react,
so fucking differently
but all inside this one body.
And I can't believe that somebody
I barely know
can throw
everything into such chaos.

An internal world
of infernal tornadoes,
fiercely whirling with
raging rainbows.

Rage glows
red.
And my heart explodes
the colour of passion.

And it turns out the two
can be easily mistaken.

As my head explodes
and blows its load,
words the colour of lava
flow
down
the volcano
of me.

Orangey,
yellow,
molten words,
fade to grey
as the flow slows
and the stone grows
cool and hard -
like his heart
after the heat goes.

He grows green
with jealousy,
as I'm seen
'overzealously
enjoying the company
of another human being.'

Apparently.

I grow green
with sickness,
as I witness –

him,

switch to violet.

A silent, violent demeanour.

He's getting meaner.
Which, I know
should mean our
friendship is over,
but it's hard to go
as I watch him shift to indigo,
then blue.

My heart hurts to feel this hue.

Sadness -
is a heavy colour.
And carrying it for too long drove me to madness.

My colours could no longer coexist.

The passion. The pain.
The guilt. The grief.
The jealousy. The joy.
The rage. The relief.
The sorrow. The shock.
The doubt. The disbelief.
The denial. The despair.
The hope and new belief.

It was all too much to contain in one vessel,
and though I wrestled and tried to resist -
I split.

I am rainbow now.

The result of sun co-existing with rain.
Joy, co-existing with pain.

The ghost of him haunts me still.

But I'll let myself cry,
then let the light shine
and spill my colours in the sky.

Did I mention I was best friends with a butterfly?

I watched in awe as she dissolved in the darkness before emerging fabulous and free.

She –

Flutters in and out of my life.

But I'm grateful for that.

Butterflies do not belong in cages.

Facebook, Instagram, YouTube: @ClaireTedstoneArt

ACKNOWLEDGEMENTS

To the phenomenal poetry community of who there are too many names to mention. If you think this is about you, it is. Thank you for sharing your stories with me and for listening to mine. Ya'll are life savers.

Thank you to Stuart, Verve Poetry Press and Verve Poetry Festival for the endless support and opportunities you provide to myself and fellow artists.

Stefan, thank you for accepting every single aspect of me exactly as we are, thank you for the safety and for always waiting for me to come back. You are all love and I love all of you all the much.

Mum and Dad, no others compare. Constantly learning and updating your views on everything to understand us all. Thank you for helping me to grow and being glad to grow with me. The world would be an easier place with more as willing as you.

My brothers, Chris, Matt and Rick, thank you for our relationships which are all so different but all equally as important and loving.

Thank you to Freya, Barney and Walter for being fresh air when I can't breathe, light when I'm heavy, honest when the world isn't and fun when life gets serious.

Nanna, 100 years strong. Thank you for teaching us and loving us.

Jordan Boyd, thank you for all the love and laughs. We love you and we miss you every day.

James and Claire, thank you for your stunning poem contributions and your beautiful friendships. I can't wait for more collaborations with you both.

Tim, thank you for the book cover and just thank you, continuously, forever.

Donnie Barker, my bestie, we've been through it all together despite not being together. Thank you for a friendship that transcends 4000 miles.

Becky, my (most recent) therapist, you changed my life. You would say it was all me but that's why you're so good at what you do. Thank you for everything.

Sunny, you are sunshine to everyone else even on your darkest days. Thank you for being exactly who you are.

Yogasweat Birmingham, thank you to a beautiful team of people for the safest space.

The Word Association, thank you for giving me the opportunity to host Speak Your Mind at The Old Needleworks Foundation in Redditch.

Thank you to Apples and Snakes for commissioning me to write 'Train', a poem on the subject of environment.

Thank you to Verve Poetry Festival for commissioning me to write 'Dust', a poem on the subject of diversity for the anthology *We've Done Nothing Wrong, We've Nothing To Hide* published by Verve Poetry Press.

Thank you to Mouthpieces and FOLIO Sutton Coldfield for commissioning me to write 'Shakespeare', a poem on the subject of Shakespeare for his birthday week in 2022.

Dan, thank you for coming to me with the concept for 'His Name Is...' and leaving me free to run wild with it.

Quotes in 'Jemanji' are accredited to the film Jumanji, 1995.

ALSO AVAILABLE FROM VERVEPOETRYPRESS.COM

Unorthodox
Jemima Hughes

The stunning debut collection from Jemima - starting her poetry career with an explosion!

Jemima Hughes brings you her first autobiographical poetry collection which will sweep you up and drag you through the "mindfield" of the 'Unorthodox'. Whilst tearing through experiences of abuse and mental health, Jemima leads you into a whirlwind of love and heartbreak, providing a raw and relatable outlet.

Sometimes a tornado can be more beautiful than it is destructive, either way it will keep you gripped.

'You are destined to win this war ... because you are the only one in it.'

Jemima's powerful debut is the perfect companion to her wonderful follow-up, *Into The Ordinary*!

Available in paperback:
ISBN: 978 1 912565 38 2
78 pages • 216 x 138 • 30 poems
£9.99

And on eBook:
ISBN: 978 1 912565 91 7
£6.49

ALSO AVAILABLE FROM VERVEPOETRYPRESS.COM

Eighty Four:
Poems on Male Suicide, Vulnerability, Grief and Hope

With an introduction from editor Helen Calcutt

Eighty Four was originally a new anthology of poetry on the subject of male suicide in aid of CALM. Poems were donated to the collection by Andrew McMillan, Salena Godden, Anthony Anaxogorou, Katrina Naomi, Ian Patterson, Caroline Smith, Carrie Etter, Peter Raynard, Joelle Taylor, while a submissions window yielded many excellent poems on the subject from hitherto unknown poets we are thrilled to have been made aware of.

We hope this book will shed light on an issue that is cast in shadow, and which is often shrouded in secrecy and denial. If we don't talk, we don't heal and we don't change. In Eighty Four we are all talking. Are you listening?

Available in paperback:
ISBN: 978 1 912565 13 9
188 pages • 216 x 138 • 56 poems
£11.99

And on eBook:
ISBN: 978 1 912565 79 5
£6.99

ABOUT VERVE POETRY PRESS

Verve Poetry Press is an award-winning press that focused initially on meeting a local need in Birmingham - a need for the vibrant poetry scene here in Brum to find a way to present itself to the poetry world via publication. Co-founded by Stuart Bartholomew and Amerah Saleh, it now publishes poets from all corners of the UK - poets that speak to the city's varied and energetic qualities and will contribute to its many poetic stories.

Added to this is a colourful pamphlet series, many featuring poets who have performed at our sister festival - and a poetry show series which captures the magic of longer poetry performance pieces by festival alumni such as Polarbear, Matt Abbott and Imogen Stirling.

The press has been voted Most Innovative Publisher at the Saboteur Awards, and has won the Publisher's Award for Poetry Pamphlets at the Michael Marks Awards.

Like the festival, we strive to think about poetry in inclusive ways and embrace the multiplicity of approaches towards this glorious art.

www.vervepoetrypress.com
@VervePoetryPres
mail@vervepoetrypress.com